S0-AFK-132

Cornerstones of Freedom

Lewis and Clark

R. Conrad Stein

CHILDREN'S PRESS®
A Division of Grolier Publishing
New York • London • Hong Kong • Sydney
Danbury, Connecticut

Library of Congress Cataloging-in-Publication Data

Stein, R. Conrad.
    Lewis and Clark / R. Conrad Stein.
       p. cm.—(Cornerstones of freedom)
    Includes index.
    Summary: Describes the 1804–1806 Lewis and Clark Expedition,
which took the explorers from St. Louis to the Pacific Ocean.
    ISBN: 0-516-20461-0 (lib. bdg.)   0-516-26228-9 (pbk.)
    1. Lewis and Clark Expedition (1804–1806)—Juvenile literature.
    2. Lewis, Meriwether, 1774–1809—Juvenile literature. 3. Clark,
William, 1770–1838—Juvenile literature. [1. Lewis and Clark
Expedition (1804–1806) 2. Lewis, Meriwether, 1774–1809. 3. Clark,
William, 1770–1838. 4. Explorers.] I. Title. II. Series.
F592.7.S72   1997
917.804'2—dc21
                                                                    96-50146
                                                                         CIP
                                                                          AC

In 1803, Thomas Jefferson concluded the Louisiana Purchase with France. With the president's signature, the Louisiana Purchase doubled the size of the young United States. Before this transaction, the nation's borders stretched from the Atlantic coast to the Mississippi River. West of the Mississippi lay the region of Louisiana. Beyond Louisiana was a little-explored territory called Oregon. Jefferson believed that the nation would someday spread west all the way to the Pacific Ocean.

Thomas Jefferson (above) bought Louisiana for the United States from France for $11,250,000.

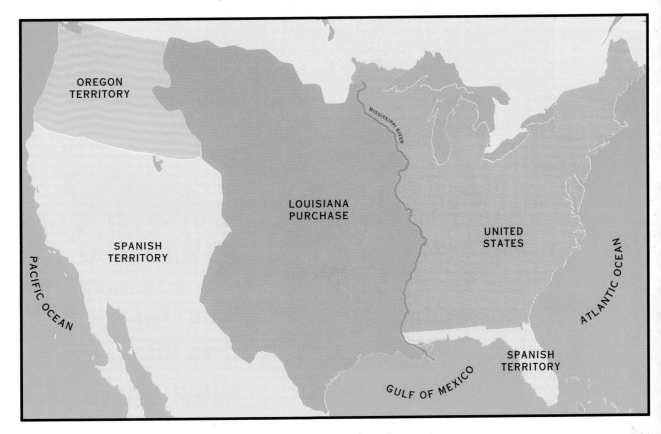

OREGON
TERRITORY

MISSISSIPPI RIVER

LOUISIANA
PURCHASE

UNITED
STATES

SPANISH
TERRITORY

PACIFIC OCEAN

ATLANTIC OCEAN

SPANISH
TERRITORY

GULF OF MEXICO

Meriwether Lewis

William Clark

But before the country could expand, Jefferson decided that American explorers must make a bold journey through Louisiana and Oregon to the Pacific shores. To head this expedition, the president chose twenty-nine-year-old Meriwether Lewis. The Lewis family was Jefferson's neighbors in Virginia, and Meriwether had once served as the president's secretary. Lewis asked his army friend, William Clark, age thirty-three, to assist him. From the beginning, the two men agreed that they would be co-captains, sharing the responsibilities of command. They also agreed to recruit about thirty men for the voyage. They called the expedition the Corps of Discovery.

In the spring of 1804, the Corps of Discovery assembled in St. Louis, Missouri, where the Missouri River meets the Mississippi River. St. Louis, a village of about one thousand people, was the last large outpost in what was then the

St. Louis, Missouri, was just a small town when the Corps of Discovery set off to explore the West.

western United States. Lewis and Clark began their voyage with three vessels. The largest craft was a keelboat with a large sail that held equipment and about twenty men. In addition, the expedition had two canoes that carried five or six men each. This tiny fleet left St. Louis on May 14, 1804. No one in the party knew when—or if—they would ever return.

Miles up the Missouri River, only the songs of birds and the splashing of oars broke the stillness. The explorers gazed at deer and elk feeding on the riverbank. Farther west, a yellow-colored doglike animal appeared and barked at the keelboat. William Clark called the animal a prairie wolf. It was the first time the explorers from the East Coast had ever seen a coyote. Fish were abundant in the Missouri River, so the party occasionally stopped to fish. One summer morning they caught 490 catfish in just a few hours.

The explorers were awed by the majestic scenery they encountered on their journey.

Despite the region's abundance and awesome beauty, exploration of the West was not easy for the travelers. Mosquitoes, flies, and gnats constantly buzzed above the expedition. Lewis wrote, "[The mosquitoes] continued to infest us in such a manner that we could scarcely exist."

The details of the Lewis and Clark expedition have been preserved in records written by the travelers. From the beginning, the two leaders wrote journals noting the sights and sounds of the western wilderness. The other explorers on the mission were also encouraged to compile diaries. This record-keeping resulted in hundreds of pages of rich accounts of the 8,000-mile (13,000-kilometer) round-trip adventure.

Woolly mammoths were long-extinct animals, but Jefferson thought they might be found in the West.

Lewis and Clark hoped to reach the villages of the Mandan and Hidatsa American Indians before the winter began. The Indian settlements were about 1,300 miles (2,100 km) from St. Louis. For more than twenty years, this part of the Missouri River had been traveled by French traders who bought beaver pelts and other furs from the Indians. The French left descriptions and some maps of the region. Still, the territory was largely unexplored and filled with mystery. Even Thomas Jefferson, who had studied the fossilized bones of prehistoric woolly mammoths, thought that the huge beasts might still roam the western lands.

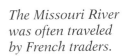

The Missouri River was often traveled by French traders.

The travelers knew that they would also encounter the Lakota, who lived along the western region of the Missouri River. The Lakota were known as fierce warriors. They sometimes fought neighboring tribes and demanded gifts from whites trading on the river. President Jefferson had written careful instructions to the Corps of Discovery about how they should regard the Lakota: "Of that nation we wish most particularly to make a friendly impression because of their immense power."

In September, the explorers spotted their first herd of pronghorn antelope. Lewis wrote, "I had this day an opportunity of witnessing the agility and superior fleetness of this animal which was to me really astonishing." Another unusual animal the party encountered was the prairie dog. The explorers marveled at the tiny city of tunnels and burrows that the prairie dogs had built in the ground.

The pronghorn antelope (left) and the black-tailed prairie dog (below) were among the animals the explorers saw for the first time on their expedition.

At the mouth of the Teton River in present-day South Dakota, the explorers met the Lakota. The encounter began peacefully. Three teenage Lakota boys swam out to the keelboat and said, through the expedition's interpreters, that the chiefs wished to speak with the explorers. Four Lakota chiefs arrived, and Lewis invited them aboard the keelboat. Lewis offered the chiefs whiskey and tobacco, commonly accepted gifts at that time. The conversation soon grew tense, however, and Lewis ordered Clark and four men to take the chiefs back to shore in one of the canoes. As Clark paddled toward the beach, one of the four chiefs became "very insolent in both words and gestures . . . stating he had not received [enough] presents," Clark wrote. At the

Although Lewis and Clark sometimes had difficult encounters with American Indians, most of their experiences with the Indians were friendly.

riverbank, a Lakota warrior grabbed the canoe's bowline (a rope that was used to tie the canoe in place) and refused to let it go. A furious William Clark drew his sword.

Lewis, watching from the keelboat, commanded his men to aim their rifles at the Lakota. The Lakota strung arrows onto their bowstrings. Tense moments passed, but what could have been a bloody fight ended with a standoff. Clark coolly took the bowline from the warrior's hands and returned to the keelboat.

Beyond the Lakota territory, the voyagers passed through the tall grasslands of the Great Plains. There the explorers saw buffalo herds that were so thick that the Plains looked black. Deer were as numerous as birds. The explorers hunted to provide meat for food. But, Lewis wrote, "Although game is very abundant and gentle, we kill only as is necessary for food."

Buffalo were abundant on the Great Plains.

As they traveled, the crew members grew to appreciate the personality differences between their leaders. Meriwether Lewis was a loner who did not like to ride in the boats. He preferred to walk along the riverbank, scouting miles ahead of the main party. William Clark, though, was a fun-loving redhead who was quick to laugh. A superb boatman, Clark navigated the keelboat through the tricky waters. Both Lewis and Clark were excellent judges of people's character. When selecting their crew before their departure from St. Louis, they were careful not to choose any potential deserters or troublemakers. As a result, Lewis and Clark finished their expedition with most of the same men they had hired at

Lewis spent many hours of the journey scouting ahead of the rest of the expedition.

the beginning. One crew member died of a fever early in the voyage, and two others had to be punished for breaking rules. But the rest worked together through the uncertainties and dangers that the expedition faced.

In the fall of 1804, the party reached the villages of the Mandan and Hidatsa Indians in what is today central North Dakota. Because they had traded with the French, the Indians were not surprised to see the light-skinned explorers. But they were amazed by a man named York, the only black member of the Corps of Discovery. Some of the Indians thought that York was a spirit. The Mandan chief believed that York was really a white man who had covered himself with black paint. York, however, was delighted by the attention he received from the tribes, and spent many hours playing with the Indians' children.

The Mandan and Hidatsa Indians were fascinated by York, the only black member of Lewis and Clark's expedition.

Lewis and Clark first met Sacagawea (center) and Toussaint Charbonneau (left of Sacagawea) at the Mandan village where they spent the winter of 1805.

While spending the winter with the Indians, the explorers met a French-Canadian trader named Toussaint Charbonneau and his wife, a sixteen-year-old Shoshone named Sacagawea. Sacagawea was captured by a rival Indian nation when she was eleven years old and was sold to Charbonneau as a slave. Eventually, they married and Sacagawea became pregnant. The couple expressed interest in leaving the camp with the expedition the

The explorers built a fort near the Mandan and Hidatsa villages where they wintered for six months.

following spring. Lewis and Clark believed that Sacagawea could assist them as a translator. They decided to take the couple with them. It proved to be a wise choice.

On April 7, 1805, the Corps of Discovery sailed out of the winter camp to resume their journey. Thus the party left the little-explored region of Louisiana and plunged into the vast territory of Oregon. They had no idea what lay ahead—perhaps they would face raging rivers, unpassable mountains, and unfriendly Indians. Earlier, Lewis and Clark had sent the keelboat with a small crew back to St. Louis. Their fleet now consisted of the two large canoes and six smaller boats that were built while wintering among the Mandan and Hidatsa Indians. Pondering his place in history, Lewis wrote, "We were now about to penetrate a country . . . on which the foot of civilized man had never trodden; the good or evil it had in store for us was for experiment yet to determine."

Lewis and Clark set out from St. Louis, Missouri, in May 1804, and they reached the Pacific Ocean in November 1805.

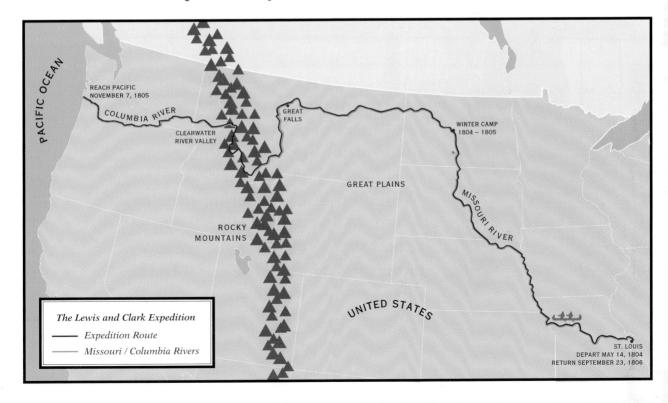

PACIFIC OCEAN

REACH PACIFIC
NOVEMBER 7, 1805

COLUMBIA RIVER

CLEARWATER
RIVER VALLEY

GREAT
FALLS

WINTER CAMP
1804 – 1805

GREAT PLAINS

MISSOURI RIVER

ROCKY
MOUNTAINS

UNITED STATES

ST. LOUIS
DEPART MAY 14, 1804
RETURN SEPTEMBER 23, 1806

The Lewis and Clark Expedition
— *Expedition Route*
— *Missouri / Columbia Rivers*

In this unexplored land, Lewis reported seeing "immense quantities of game in every direction . . . consisting of herds of buffalo, elk, and antelopes, with some deer and wolves." The land was so devoid of people that the animals had rarely been hunted and showed little fear of the party. The explorers had to throw stones at the buffalo so they could clear a path through the herd. One curious buffalo calf followed Meriwether Lewis everywhere he went.

The Mandan had warned the explorers about a species of bear that, when it stood on its hind legs, was as tall as an Indian tipi. Lewis dismissed the Mandans' story. Then, on May 11, a breathless crew member raced into camp claiming he was being chased by a monstrous bear that kept pursuing him, even though he had shot it twice. Hunters killed the bear and estimated its weight to be 600 pounds (272 kg). It was the first grizzly bear any of the explorers had seen at close range. Lewis later wrote, "I . . . would rather fight two Indians than one [of these] bears."

William Clark had perhaps the best eyesight of any crew member. On May 26, he saw the outline of a great mountain range to the west. In the next few days, all of the explorers could see the snow-covered Rocky Mountains on the horizon. The sight was inspiring as well as troubling. The explorers knew that they would have to find a way to cross the incredible barrier.

Before they could cross the Rockies, the Corps of Discovery faced the Great Falls of the Missouri River in present-day Montana. Here the river tumbled down a bluff that was as high as a modern six-story building. The roar of the water was deafening. Lewis called it, "the grandest sight I ever beheld." But the waterfall meant that the explorers had to carry their boats and supplies up steep cliffs before they could set out again on quieter waters upstream. Traveling around the falls took the party twenty-four days, and left everyone exhausted.

The Great Falls of the Missouri River were a beautiful sight, but also were difficult to travel around.

Carrying her baby boy on her back, Sacagawea won the admiration of the crew. She carefully scanned the riverbank to find edible roots and fruit. These foods provided a welcome relief from the customary diet of meat and water. And in the mountain country, the Missouri River became a crooked stream that split into many small tributaries. Sacagawea pointed out landmarks that she remembered from a journey as a slave child, and she helped the captains choose the correct river branches on which to travel.

Sacagawea quickly proved to be a valuable asset to the expedition.

Soon the members of the party began to wonder why they had not yet seen any Shoshone or other American Indians. They had seen signs of Indian settlement—hunters' trails and abandoned campsites—but since they left the Mandan and Hidatsa villages, the Corps of Discovery had not encountered any other people at all.

In mid-August, Meriwether Lewis, hiking ahead of the party with a few other explorers, came upon three Shoshone women and several children. Lewis had carried an American flag in his pack for just such a meeting. He waved the banner and walked slowly toward the group. One of the children fled. The women sat very still as if frozen with fear. Lewis explained that he was an explorer, and the women led him to their village.

At first, the Shoshone were cautious of Lewis and Clark, but the explorers soon realized that they were fortunate to encounter the Indians.

The Shoshone were a small tribe who were almost always at war with their powerful neighbors, the Blackfeet. They had never seen white people, but constant warfare made the Shoshone suspicious of all outsiders. Lewis hoped to buy horses from the tribe. Now that the rivers had all but disappeared, he needed horses to cross the peaks of the Rocky Mountains. But the chief, Cameahwait, would not part with any of the animals. Lewis did persuade Cameahwait to send a few Shoshone to find Clark and the rest of the party and bring them to the village.

The next morning, Clark and the others arrived at the village, and a meeting was held with Chief Cameahwait. Sacagawea prepared to serve as the translator. When the meeting began, Sacagawea stared intently at the chief. Then she broke into tears of joy. Lewis wrote, "She jumped up, ran, and embraced him, and threw her blanket over him, and cried profusely." Sacagawea recognized Cameahwait as her brother, whom she had not seen in six years. Cheers and laughter rose from the village. The Shoshone hailed Sacagawea as a lost daughter who had come home.

On September 1, 1805, the Corps of Discovery left the Shoshone territory. Chief Cameahwait not only provided the party with horses, he also gave them a guide to show them the best route through the mountains. Crossing the Rockies proved to be a difficult ordeal. The trails were too rugged to ride on, so the party walked and used the horses as pack animals.

In mid-September, a blinding snowstorm struck. Even the Shoshone guide got lost. Worst of all, the once-abundant wild game could not be found on the high mountain peaks. The explorers were forced to kill some of their pack animals for meat. The explorers' journals report that the men laughed out loud when they finally crossed the mountains and reached grasslands on level terrain.

Crossing the Rocky Mountains was one of the most difficult parts of the expedition. Left: Part of the trail (in Montana) the explorers used still exists. Right: The expedition crossed the Rockies on foot, using the horses to carry their equipment and supplies.

Upon reaching the Clearwater River Valley, the expedition built new canoes to continue their journey west.

The Lewis and Clark expedition emerged from the Rocky Mountains into the lovely valley of the Clearwater River in present-day Idaho. The waters were so clear that the river bottom and schools of fish were visible despite the river's depth. In the Clearwater country, Lewis and Clark abandoned their pack horses and built new canoes. They reasoned that the streams on this side of the Rockies would all eventually flow into the Columbia River, the major river of the Pacific Northwest. American Indians called the Columbia River the *Ouragon* or *Origan*. The land around it was later called the Oregon Territory.

Traveling the rivers, the voyagers met the Nez Perce Indians, who taught them valuable techniques for building and sailing log canoes. Less friendly were the Chinook, who drove hard bargains when trading for goods. But encountering the Chinook meant that the Pacific Ocean was not far away. One of the Chinook wore a black navy coat that he may have bought from a North American or European sailor.

The explorers experienced some difficulty in dealing with the Chinook Indians, but their encounter brought signs that the Pacific Ocean was near.

A dismal rain pelted the travelers in early November as they sailed down the Columbia River. They made a camp near an Indian village and spent a restless night. On the morning of November 7, 1805, the rain stopped and the fog cleared. A chorus of shouts suddenly went up from the camp. William Clark scribbled in his notes, "Ocean in view! O! the joy." On the horizon, still many miles to the west, lay the great Pacific Ocean. Upon seeing the ocean, some of the explorers wept, and others said prayers of thanksgiving.

But arriving at the Pacific Ocean did not end the Lewis and Clark expedition. The party still had to return home to St. Louis. President Jefferson had provided Meriwether Lewis with

The explorers saw the Pacific Ocean for the first time near present-day Astoria, Oregon.

a letter of credit guaranteeing payment to any ship captain who would take the explorers to the eastern coast. The party made a winter camp at the mouth of the Columbia River near present-day Astoria, Oregon, and kept a watch for ships. No vessels were spotted. Finally, on March 23, 1806, the crew broke camp and began the long trek east toward St. Louis.

Jefferson's letter of credit survived the journey west, but it was never used because the explorers returned home overland, instead of by ship.

To the explorers, the six-month return journey seemed to be easier than their first journey because they knew what to expect in the river and mountain country. When the crew reached the Mandan village, they said good-bye to Sacagawea and her husband and continued back to St. Louis.

Sacagawea is remembered as a vital reason for the success of the Lewis and Clark expedition. This statue of Sacagawea stands in Bismarck, North Dakota.

On September 23, 1806, the Lewis and Clark expedition arrived safely back in St. Louis, Missouri, where their journey had begun more than two years earlier. The travelers had gone a distance of just less than 4,000 miles (6,400 km) from St. Louis to the mouth of the Columbia River and back. But the twisting rivers and mountain trails meant that the Corps of Discovery had actually covered about 8,000 miles (13,000 km) on the history-making trip. Throughout the explorers' travels, they encountered more than fifty American-Indian tribes. The expedition returned with numerous samples of plant and animal life that had never before been seen by American scientists. Before the expedition, President Jefferson had hoped that the explorers would find a broad river that ships could use to sail directly to the Pacific Ocean. Lewis and Clark failed to find such a river, and the expedition was final proof that an inland waterway in North America did not exist.

HISTORY

OF

THE EXPEDITION

UNDER THE COMMAND OF

CAPTAINS LEWIS AND CLARK,

TO

THE SOURCES OF THE MISSOURI,

THENCE

ACROSS THE ROCKY MOUNTAINS

AND DOWN THE

RIVER COLUMBIA TO THE PACIFIC OCEAN.

PERFORMED DURING THE YEARS 1804—5—6.

By order of the

GOVERNMENT OF THE UNITED STATES.

PREPARED FOR THE PRESS

BY PAUL ALLEN, ESQUIRE.

IN TWO VOLUMES.

VOL. I.

PHILADELPHIA:
PUBLISHED BY BRADFORD AND INSKEEP; AND
ABM. H. INSKEEP, NEWYORK.
J. Maxwell, Printer.
1814.

The journals kept by Captains Lewis, Clark, and several members of their expedition have been compiled into many published accounts since the journey ended in 1806. This one, published in 1814, was printed in two volumes.

From St. Louis, Lewis and Clark traveled to Washington, D.C. Almost every town they passed through brought out bands to welcome them as heroes. In Washington, D.C., the explorers delighted President Jefferson with tales of grizzly bears and high mountain passes. The president said, "Lewis and Clark have entirely fulfilled my expectations. . . . The world will find that those travelers have well earned its favor."

The Lewis and Clark expedition is commemorated by many historic sites along the route the explorers traveled.

To Meriwether Lewis and William Clark, the mission itself was their greatest reward. Traveling through virtually unexplored lands was an exhilarating experience that they would cherish for the rest of their lives. Although they faced many dangers, the thrill—not the peril— of the expedition bursts from the pages of the journals they kept. As Lewis wrote the day he left the Indian village to enter the Western wilderness, "I could but esteem this moment of my departure as among the most happy of my life."

GLOSSARY

agility – ability to move quickly and easily

devoid – lacking or without

exhilarating – exciting and thrilling

expedition – long march or journey taken for a specific purpose

fossilized – to become preserved as rock

game – wild animals that are hunted for food

insolent – insulting or arrogant

journal

journal – written record

keelboat – large, flat-bottomed boat used for travel on rivers

mammoth – species of elephant-like animal that lived
during the Ice Age

outpost – remote settlement

pelted – to be struck repeatedly

mammoth

transaction – an exchange of goods, services, or money

trod – to walk or to step on

TIMELINE

1770 William Clark born

1774 Meriwether Lewis born

1775

Revolutionary War {

1783

Sacagawea born **1788**

1801 Thomas Jefferson becomes president

1803 Louisiana Purchase

1804

1805

May: Corps of
Discovery leaves
St. Louis

June:
Expedition
reaches Great
Falls (Montana)

1806 *September:* Expedition returns to St. Louis

1809 Meriwether Lewis dies

October:
Explorers meet
Sacagawea

November:
Expedition
reaches
Pacific Ocean

1812 Reported death of Sacagawea

William Clark dies **1838**

INDEX (**Boldface** *page numbers indicate illustrations.*)

PHOTO CREDITS

©: Courtesy of Amon Carter Museum, Fort Worth, Texas: 23 (painting by Charles Russell); Corbis-Bettmann: 18; Dembinsky Photo Assoc.: 9 top (Mike Barlow); Independence National Historical Park: 3, 4, 31 top right; James P. Rowan: 9 bottom; Missouri Historical Society: 4 bottom, 6, 25, 30 top, 31 left; Courtesy of Montana Historical Society: 1, 13; North Wind Picture Archives: 5, 7 bottom, 10, 21 left, 27; State Historical Society of North Dakota: 14 top, 26, 31 bottom right; Steve Bly: 22; Steve Terrill: 24; Stock Montage, Inc.: 14 bottom (The Newberry Library), 12, 21 right; Superstock, Inc.: cover, 7 top, 8, 11, 19, 30 bottom; Thomas Gilcrease Institute of American History and Art, Tulsa, Oklahoma: 17 (Painting by O.C. Seltzer); Tom Stack & Associates: 16 (John Shaw); Tom Till: 2; Unicorn Stock Photos: 28 (Andre Jenny).

Maps by TJS Design.

ABOUT THE AUTHOR

R. Conrad Stein was born in Chicago, Illinois. After serving in the Marine Corps he attended the University of Illinois, where he received a degree in history. He later studied in Mexico, where he received an advanced degree. A full-time writer, Mr. Stein has published more than eighty books for young readers. He lives in Chicago with his wife and their daughter, Janna.